"This book provides actionable exercises t[...] anxiety. Instead of reading dry text, the r[...] blank' exercises throughout the book. Lear[...] Many self-help books have exercises, but *Put Your Anxiety Here* is unique in offering a variety of easy-to-do exercises cover to cover."

—**Edmund J. Bourne, PhD**, former director of The Anxiety Treatment Center in Santa Rosa, CA; and author of *The Anxiety and Phobia Workbook*

"Successful therapy is hard work, typically provided by seeing a therapist. Lisa Schab's journal provides what it promises: a gentle but direct alternative approach to find calm. Schab makes it fun and provides a process toward self-awareness and goal attainment. 'Therapy that doesn't look like therapy.' I think it's a valuable addition to any professional treatment plan, leaving the feeling, *you did it.*"

—**Ronald D. Groat, MD**, board-certified psychiatrist, and past president of the Minnesota Psychiatric Society

"Lisa Schab's book is a must-have for mental health clinicians. The book consists primarily of well-designed worksheets that engage the client in their own healing. Clients acquire a sense of control over their emotional well-being as they secure a set of mental health tools to be used throughout their lifetime. The book is grounded in sound psychological theory, backed by extensive experience, and best of all—it works!"

—**Lynn R. Moosman, MA, LCPC**, psychotherapist, supervisor of graduate students at The Family Institute at Northwestern University, and former director of clinical services at Youth & Family Counseling

"I LOVE this book, and wish I had it for clients when I began my practice years ago. It is wise, practical, creative, and healing without being threatening. I especially value the holistic approach involving breathing, movement, drawing, music, and imagination. It is also important that the suggestions, though seeming whimsical at times, are scientifically based. I highly recommend this book for individual or group use."

—**Barbara Blake, RSM, MA**, artist, teacher, and psychotherapist with thirty years of experience

"Schab's *Put Your Anxiety Here* offers the ultimate collection of writing prompts to better understand anxiety using a creative and insight-oriented approach. The wide-ranging, evidence-based journal topics have a broad appeal for mindfully examining anxiety in all forms, and provide space for addressing intense emotions, unhelpful cognitions, and physical symptoms of anxiety. The book is an excellent resource for individual exploration or adjunctive use in counseling."

> —David H. Klemanski, PsyD, MPH, assistant professor of psychiatry at
> Yale University, and coauthor of *Don't Let Your Anxiety Run Your Life*

"I have known Lisa Schab for many years and have known her to be a gifted writer and therapist. I am very pleased to have a journal written by her that I can recommend to my adult patients. Anxiety is at the root of so many of our health issues today, and this journal provides helpful exercises to ease its effects."

> —Karen Judy, MD, internal medicine physician for Northwestern Medicine

"Suffering from mild to debilitating anxiety? Lisa Schab's *Put Your Anxiety Here* is a gift in self-care. Filled to the brim with exercises, this book helps to manage—and take your life back—from anxiety. Schab offers practical tools to encourage awareness, intention, grounding, and distraction—all to help alleviate troublesome physiological, emotional, and cognitive symptoms. Use this book to create a self-care plan, and don't forget to include the *joy-and-pleasure alphabet!*"

> —Diane Havnen-Smith, LCSW, psychotherapist in private practice
> in Portland, OR

"*Put Your Anxiety Here* is wonderful workbook that guides the reader through the complexities of anxiety with a soothing, down-to-earth, playful approach. Lisa Schab offers multimodal strategies including breath work, creative writing, sensory exploration, art, and grounding techniques. The reader is gently inspired to work through their symptoms by engaging their thoughts and senses to gain control of their anxiety."

> —Julie Greiner-Ferris, LICSW, senior director at Riverside Community Care,
> and coauthor of *The Yoga-CBT Workbook for Anxiety*

PUT YOUR

A CREATIVE GUIDED JOURNAL TO

ANXIETY

RELIEVE STRESS & FIND CALM

HERE

LISA M. SCHAB, LCSW

New Harbinger Publications, Inc.

Publisher's Note

This publication is designed to provide accurate and authoritative information in regard to the subject matter covered. It is sold with the understanding that the publisher is not engaged in rendering psychological, financial, legal, or other professional services. If expert assistance or counseling is needed, the services of a competent professional should be sought.

NEW HARBINGER PUBLICATIONS is a registered trademark of New Harbinger Publications, Inc.

New Harbinger Publications is an employee-owned company.

Copyright © 2023 by Lisa Schab
New Harbinger Publications, Inc.
5674 Shattuck Avenue
Oakland, CA 94609
www.newharbinger.com

Cover and interior design by Amy Shoup. Illustration work by Sara Christian.
Acquired by Tesilya Hanauer

Library of Congress Cataloging-in-Publication Data on file

Printed in the United States of America

25   24   23

10   9   8   7   6   5   4   3   2   1   First Printing

for Ellen

with love

BEGIN HERE

"

I'm frightened all the time. Scared to death. But I've never let it stop me. Never!

—GEORGIA O'KEEFE

"

No matter who you are or where you go, anxiety may find you. It can feel annoying, overwhelming, or anything in between. But however it hits you, it does *not* have to knock you down or keep you down. Nobody likes anxiety, but it doesn't have to ruin or run your life!

The prompts in this book are designed to help you let it out, let it go, and let some light in! They can help you both beat anxiety in the moment and manage it over time. Some amount of anxiety is just a normal part of life on the planet, but even though we can't get rid of it completely, we don't have to let it keep us from finding joy or reaching our dreams.

So, come to these pages with a hopeful heart, an open mind, and a sense of possibility. You *can* manage anxiety!

Here are some tips for your journey:

1. **Try not to judge yourself for feeling anxious!** Anxiety loves to feed on itself, so feeling anxious about feeling anxious will only make you feel more anxious.

> *Try to take a breath and accept the feeling.*
> *Only then can you let it go.*

2. **The writing prompts on these pages are just that—*prompts*.** They're here to start you off, but where you go from there is up to you! So, it's OK to write when it says draw, cut when it says paste, or wiggle around in whatever direction feels good!

3. **There are no "right" answers in here.** Follow the prompts by following your heart. You can't do them wrong! Trust your intuition to guide you toward whatever you need to express.

4. **Be aware** that if any prompt feels like it's *raising* your anxiety, you don't have to do it! This can happen, but don't worry. If you try on a prompt and it doesn't fit well, just keep looking until you find a better one. You can always try the first one again later, OR you can scribble it out and do something else with the page.

5. **Try to let go and play a little.** Cast off those shackles of adulting! Take a break from responsibility and let yourself flow into these pages with a sense of release and a bit of fun.

1. List all the English class writing rules you can think of:

_____

_____

_____

_____

_____

_____

_____

_____

_____

Now, cross them all out! None of them are necessary here!

2.

List all the bad things you've ever heard about anxiety:

_____

_____

_____

_____

_____

_____

_____

_____

_____

_____

_____

Cross these out, too! In this book,
your anxiety can lead you to something good!

3. Stand up and shake yourself out! (Yes, seriously.) Do the Hokey Pokey, turn yourself around, twist and shout, dance like no one's watching, wiggle like a kid—whatever helps you to loosen up!

4. Write or draw what you're thinking or feeling right now. No rules, no wrong answers!

5. Breathe … smile … and open your mind to relief…

IMPORTANT NOTE: Despite any creative whimsy or silliness you may find in these pages, please keep in mind that all the prompts in this book are based in clinical anxiety management theory. So, you'll be learning real anxiety management techniques while you doodle and express yourself. We call it "therapy that doesn't look like therapy." **Enjoy!**

You come home to find a note on your fridge.

I've left you and I'm never coming back! Don't try to find me.

Signed,
Your Anxiety

What do you feel ... and what will you do ...?

The Joy-and-Pleasure Alphabet

Write something that makes you smile for each letter.

A _____

B _____

C _____

D _____

E _____

F _____

G _____

H _____

I _____

J _____

K _____

L _____

M

N

O

P

Q

R

S

T

U

V

W

X

Y

Z

Clean out the closets of your brain. What old, unwanted, anxious thoughts can you get rid of? Make a pile here:

Breathe and trace: It's going to be OK. It's going to be OK. It's going to be OK. It's going to be OK.

It's going to be OK.

It's going

It's going to be OK.

It's going to be OK.

to be OK.

IT'S GOING TO BE OK.

On a raft ... floating down an island stream ... blossoms drop in the water around you ...

dappled sunlight ... birdsong ...

Write or draw ...

> *If nothing ever changed there would be no butterflies.*
> —PROVERB

What change are you struggling with right now?

_____

_____

_____

_____

_____

_____

What butterfly outcomes might emerge from it ...?

Cover each of these gray clouds with white paint or Liquid Paper. (Or, transform them with your favorite colors and designs.) Take your time ...

PEACE OF MIND

Place your order here ...

DRIVE-THROUGH

MENU

Find a picture of yourself feeling exceptionally joy-filled or relaxed.
Tape it here. Decorate the space around it while you relive the feeling ...

What's happening from your anxious perspective?

What's happening from your calm perspective?

Comfortable position.

Eyes closed. Deep breath.

Imagine the warmth of the sun

on your body ... feel each tense

muscle melting like butter.

FILL THIS SPACE WITH CALM.

You wake up in
the morning and
find out all your
responsibilities
have been taken
care of for you.
**Describe your
day off ...**

Listen to the song, "Don't Worry, Be Happy."
Write the best lines here ... again and again!

File your **worry thoughts** in the correct folder: Fact or Fiction

FACT

_____

_____

_____

_____

_____

_____

_____

_____

FICTION

This is the sweet, small bud
of your SERENITY FLOWER.
Imagine what it would look like in full
bloom. Show it here in all its beauty.

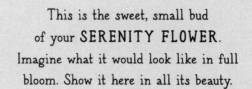

Recliner ... tub ... bed ... hammock ... pier ... deck ... forest bench ...

Bring this book to a place that feels good.

Record the peace.

What feels WAY TOO BIG to handle right now?

Break it down into all of its smaller parts.

Choose just one to tackle
first ... when you're ready.

Destination

WILDEST DREAMS

Travel Snacks

Stops Along the Way

Who's With You

Vehicle

ROAD TRIP!

Play List

Other Pleasures

43

Who (or what) has

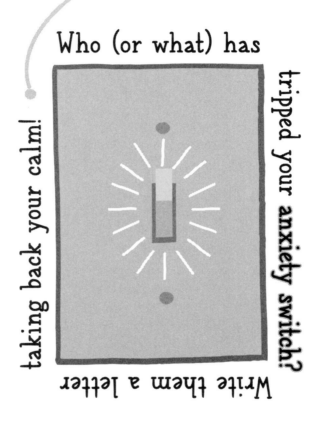

tripped your anxiety switch?

Write them a letter

taking back your calm!

BIRTH

TODAY

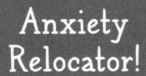

Anxiety Relocator!

1. *Deeply* inhale.

2. Completely exhale your anxious energy all across these pages!

3. CLOSE THE BOOK.

4. Go outside and shake it out into the sky.

5. Draw or write your freedom ... (Or ... leave the pages blank!)

Change your name to something peaceful. Design your nametag here.

MY NAME IS:

Which childhood wounds still fuel your anxiety?

Write healing words over or around them.

Cover each with a Band-Aid.

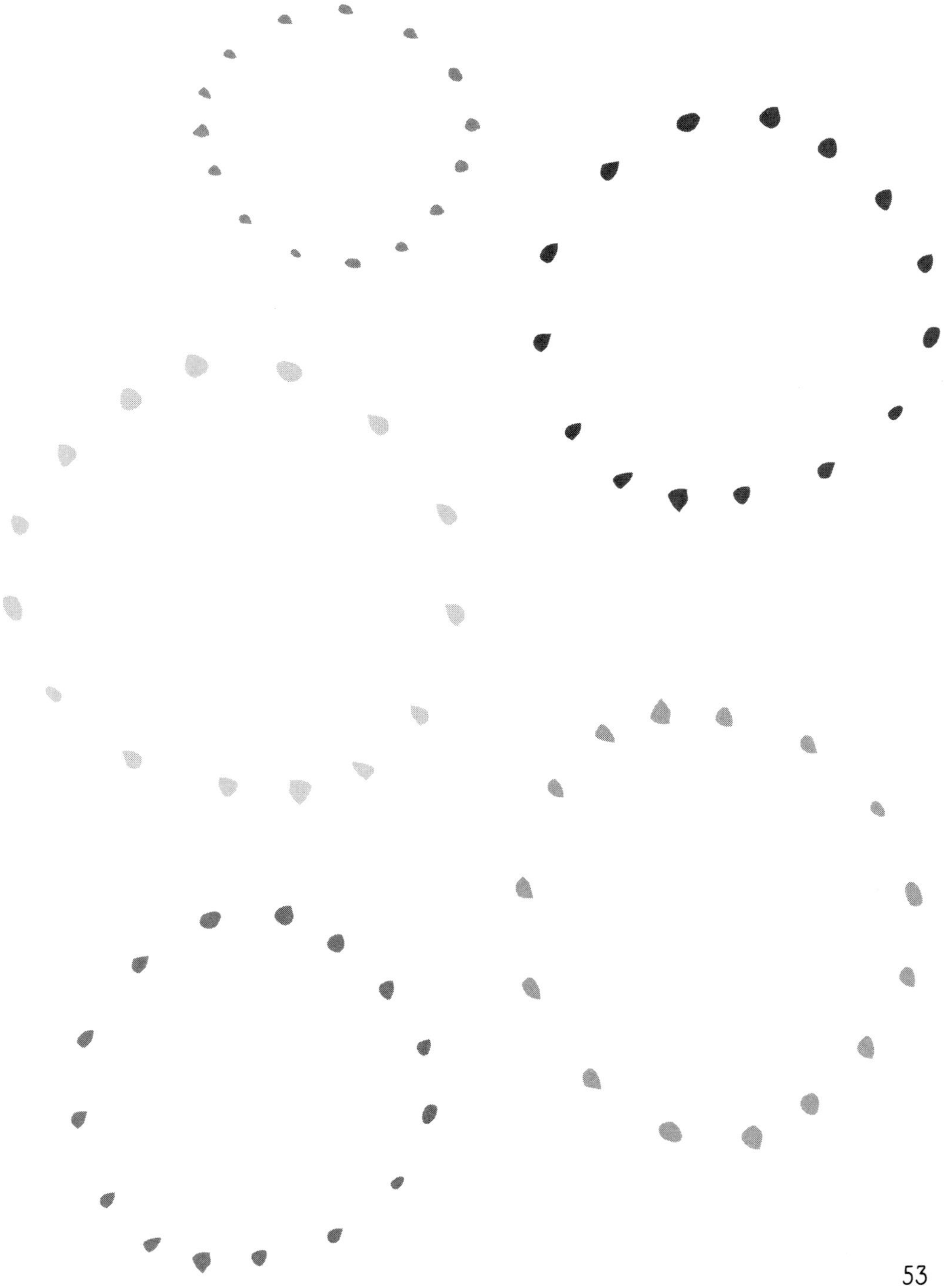

This page:
What you're feeling pressure to get done quickly:

This page:

What needs—and only what *really* needs—to get done today:

"

Excellence does not require perfection.

—PROVERB

"

EXCEL

LENCE

Color using your
nondominant hand.

Gaze at the emptiness within this circle.
Let your mind clear. When a thought enters, jot a word from
it outside the circle. Then move back to the empty space.

Breathe and repeat.
Breathe and repeat.
Breathe and repeat.

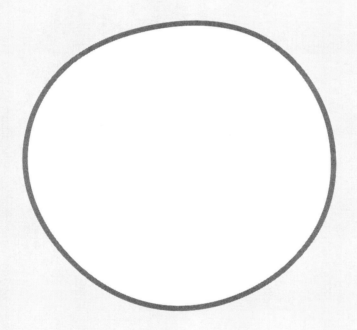

Who do you know who is hurting?

Describe a random act of kindness you could do for them.

Do it now.

YOUR ANXIOUS THOUGHT:

What would it be like if your brain NEVER had that thought again?

You run *The Peaceful Times* magazine.

Write your **Letter from the Editor** for this month's edition...

From the
EDITOR

(color draw design glue tape
add subtract cut create)

67

Lie on your back on the floor ... eyes closed ... palms up ... deep breaths.

Draw or write what you feel.

Allow yourself to feel thoroughly supported.

MESSAGES FROM YOUR ANXIOUS MIND:

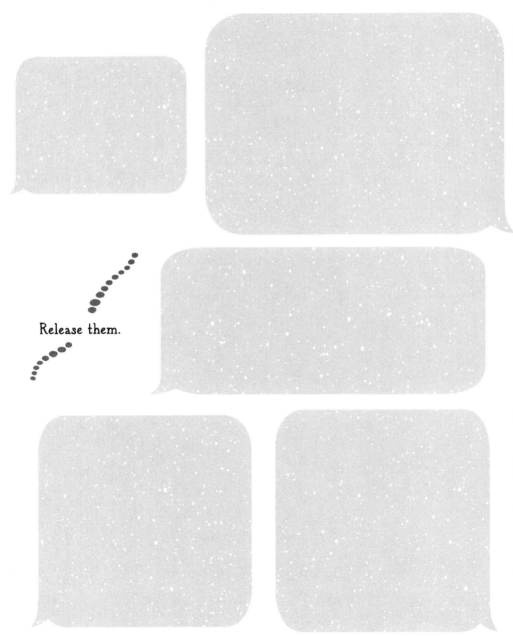

Release them.

MESSAGES FROM THE
ESSENTIAL GOODNESS IN THE UNIVERSE:

Embrace them.

DRAW YOUR MAP TO PEACE.

List anything you can be grateful for right now ...

(Colors? Windows? Pillows? Toes? Loved ones? I can breathe? I can read? I don't have to finish this prompt if I don't want to!?)

Try to find 50. Or more.

_____

1. _____

2. _____

3. _____

4. _____

5. _____

6. _____

7. _____

8. _____

9. _____

10. _____

11. _____

12. _____

13. _____

14. _____

15. _____

16. _____

17. _____

18. _____

19. _____

20. _____

21. _____

22. _____

23. _____

24. _____

25. _____

26. _____

27. _____

28. _____

29. _____

30. _____

31. _____

32. _____

33. _____

34. _____

35. _____

36. _____

37. _____

38. _____

39. _____

40. _____

41. _____

42. _____

43. _____

44. _____

45. _____

46. _____

47. _____

48. _____

49. _____

50. _____

HOLD THIS BOOK.

To the count of 3, inhale
and tighten your grip as
intensely as possible.

Squeeze your fingers, hands, arms,
shoulders, chest, and jaw.

To the count of 5, exhale
and release it all.

Repeat until your body
feels relaxed.

List the anxious thoughts that are stressing you:

TEAR OUT THIS PAGE
AND SHRED IT!!

10

9

8

7

6

5

4

3

2

1

0

Circle the number that shows how high your anxiety is right now.

Close your eyes and breathe it down a notch. Circle your new number.

Close your eyes and breathe it down again. Repeat until you're at a 2 or less.

Describe ... draw ... and dip into the vision of what's coming around the bend that you're SO looking forward to!

Here is the nest you long for ...

Fill it with whatever makes you feel safe ... stable ... secure ...

SCAVENGER HUNT!

Find and affix here:
a toothpick, a penny, a brush bristle,
the corner of a photograph, a dash of
pepper, a bit of dust from your car
dashboard, a loose thread, a price tag,
a bit of your breath, a thumbprint.

Whose problem is stressing you that really is not yours to solve?

(Friend's marriage ... Child's job struggle ... Sister's loneliness ...?)

Unpack it here and then repeat: "This does not belong to me." "This does not belong to me." "This does not belong to me."

bath / shower

sweet / salty

jeans / sweats

music / silence

book / movie

text / talk

walk / ride

comedy / drama

indoors / outdoors

forest / ocean

sandals / sneakers

rock / pop

Circle the one that feels best.

play / watch

fall / spring

formal / casual

mountains / desert

fast / slow

meat / veggies

home / away

cola / clear

city / country

train / plane

Tell more about your favorites.

Enjoy one of these now.

As you color ... breathe in peace ... breathe out love ...

On each ray of
the setting sun,
write one anxious
thought you want to
sink away.

On each ray of
the rising sun, write one
positive, peaceful thought
you want to shine through
the rest of your day.

93

Far below your thoughts is a deep well of peace ...

Close your eyes ... and go there now.
Draw or describe it ...

HOW TO ESCAPE AN ANXIETY TRAP:

STEP 1: Sit up slowly.

STEP 2: Take five deep,
gentle breaths.

STEP 3: Describe four beautiful
things you see.

STEP 4: Forgive yourself for
having a moment.

STEP 5: Move on.

Design your all-inclusive private resort on **Serenity Island**.

View:

Serenity Island

Spa amenities:

Luxury rooms:

Activities:

Tiki bar:

Menus:

Visualize yourself there now.

Your favorite childhood pet ... or toy ...

Remember them here.

Anxiety Re-Leaf ...

Fill each leaf with soothing lines and colors.

YOU'RE FLOATING ON A CLOUD ...

What stresses have you left far below? - - -

HIGH ABOVE THE EARTH.

- - - How big are they now?

Choose an event from your past that created high anxiety.

_____

_____

Rewrite your story with
the ending you would
have preferred.

> *A bird can soar because he takes himself lightly ...*
> —AUTHOR UNKNOWN

What weight can you let go of today to help you soar?

Closed eyes. Peaceful breath.

Imagine slipping your toes into warm sand …
or warm socks … or warm water …

Soak up the peace and describe it here.

Design a room where you would feel intensely peaceful.

Tape or draw
a picture
of yourself
in there.

Listen to a recording of rain … waves … birds … a waterfall …
or other sounds that soothe you … while you write or color …

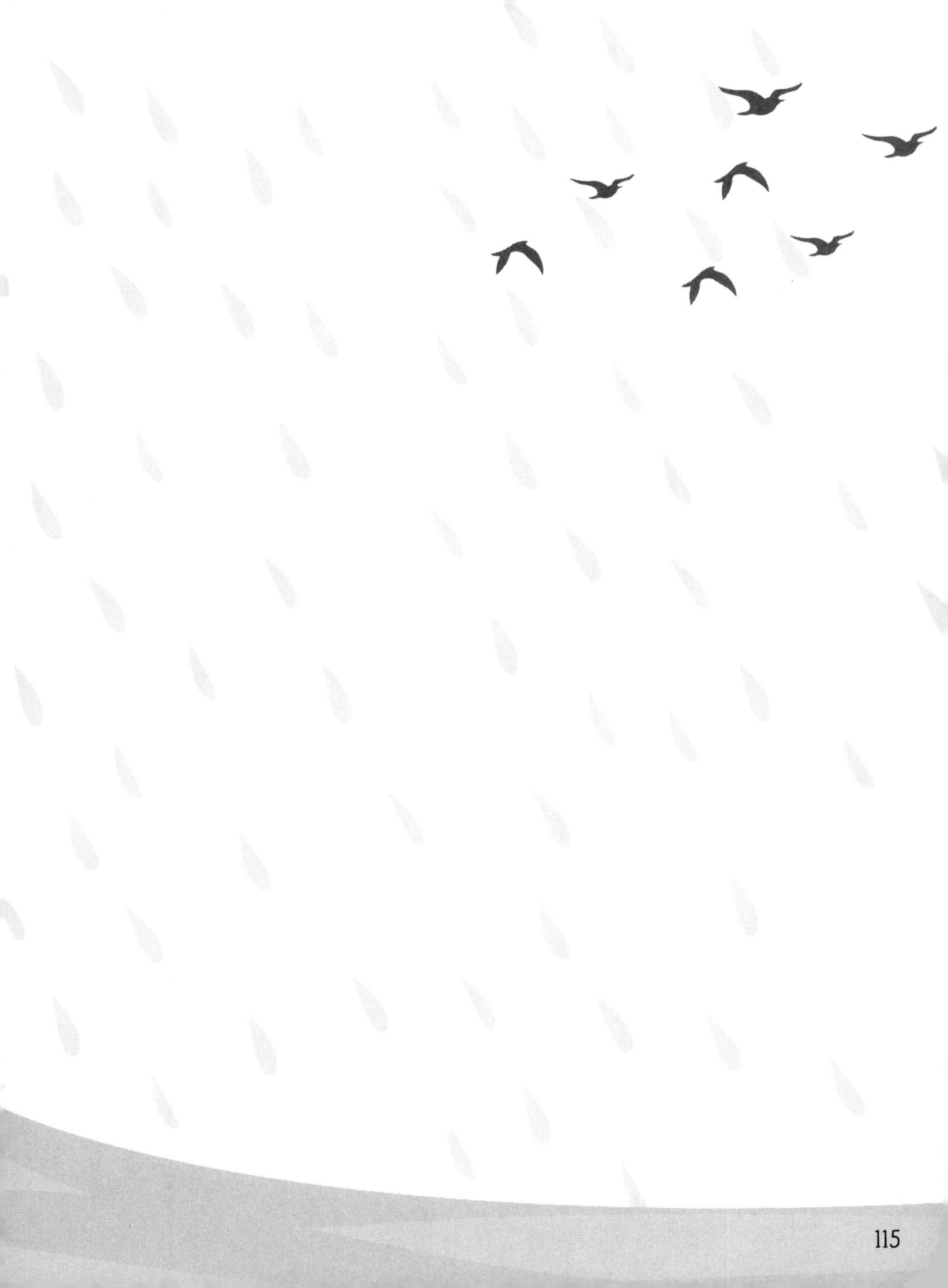

All the facets of adulthood that fuel your anxiety ... Spill them here ...

SAY THESE OUT LOUD
3 TO 5 TIMES, FAST:

A black bug's blood

Toy boat

Greek grapes

She sees cheese

The Sheik's sixth sick sheep

(Share with a child or a friend!)

DRAW SILLINESS!

Breath Massage ...

Show your anxiety "hot spots" with colors or words:

joints

jaw

back

chest

head

neck

arms

legs

stomach

face

forehead

Eyes closed,
breathe slowly and
deeply into each
tense area until
it relaxes.

Instead of floral scents, the plants in your garden all emit serenity.
Draw them here. Draw yourself in the garden.

Describe what you're overly attached to (and why).

Sit quietly ... Palms up ... Breathe ... Let it go ...

ROOTS

Which people ... places ... things ... activities ... ground you?

You've been awarded a **Nobel Inner Peace Prize**. Write your acceptance speech.

Smiling tells the brain all is well.

Draw or tape
different smiles
all over
these pages.

Try some
on yourself.

Describe in detail ... the most soothing and calming ... sight ... sound ... smell ... taste ... touch ... you can imagine.

Sight ...

Sound ...

Smell ...

Taste ...

Touch ...

You're in the ring with your anxiety.
Show yourself clearly winning the match!

135

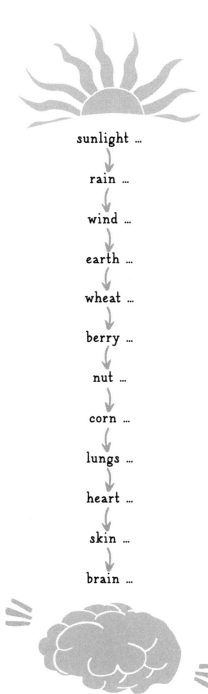

sunlight ...

rain ...

wind ...

earth ...

wheat ...

berry ...

nut ...

corn ...

lungs ...

heart ...

skin ...

brain ...

Go back to your beginning ... How does it feel to be sunlight ...?

List the insignificant things that raise your anxiety.

Then breathe
as you color ...

IT
DOESN'T
MATTER.

That time you laughed so hard you cried!
Retell the story here ...

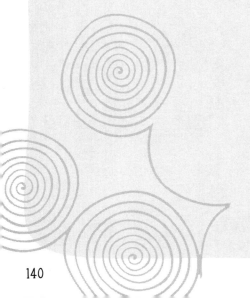

Tape or
draw a
picture
of your
anxious
inner
child
here.

Tape or
draw a
picture
of your
calm
mature
self
here.

Write a loving letter
from your calm self ⟶ to your anxious child.

Dismantle Your Anxious Thought

(Thought here:)

_____

_____

Now . . .

Write it backwards!

_____

_____

Write it upside down!

_____

_____

Change the order of the words!

_____

_____

Change the order of the letters in the words!

_____

_____

List all the vowels here:

_____

_____

List all the consonants here:

_____

_____

Make **new words** out of those letters!

_____

_____

Who's in charge now?

☐ Me

☐ Anxious Thought

145

What's happening in this moment?

COLORS

SOUNDS

SHAPES

TEXTURES

> When you feel anxious, let yourself know
> that in your mind you've moved into the future
> to something scary and your body has gotten up the
> energy for it. Come back to the present.
>
> —CHERRY HARTMAN

OBJECTS IN VIEW

EMOTIONAL FEELINGS

SCENTS/FRAGRANCES

PHYSICAL FEELINGS

TASTES

GOOD THINGS

Design a peaceful
home screen wallpaper
for your mind!

Feeling completely safe and secure,

you follow a moonlit path ...

Night-blooming flowers guide your way to a clearing ...

and a gold box that holds a message of wisdom just for you.

It says ...

Message of Wisdom

Put your anxious thoughts in the river …

Draw lines of current over and over and over them.

Remember your most beloved teacher or mentor.

What were they like?

What would they tell you now?

STRESS and **WORRY** keep calling.

For the next 5 minutes,
don't pick up!

Play here instead ...

Look at something relaxing and fill this space with words that describe it.

Try arranging the words in the shape of what you're describing ...

IT'S YOUR IDEAL DAY FIVE YEARS FROM NOW.

DESCRIBE EVERYTHING!

Draw or write a calming message on this stone ...

Then repeat it on a real stone ...

and leave it on a path for someone else to find.

1.

Write or draw your
worry thoughts in
the corners of
these pages.

2.

Fold the corners
inward to cover
the thoughts.

3.

Tape or glue
each corner
soundly shut!

WHAT TO DO NEXT

> **"**
>
> *That the birds of worry and care fly above your head, this you cannot change. But that they build nests in your hair, this you can prevent.*
>
> —CHINESE PROVERB
>
> **"**

CONGRATULATIONS!

You've just spent some time giving
yourself the gift of self-care.
This is the way out of anxiety!

To keep that gift going, take a moment to take stock.
Which type of prompts worked best for you? Those that helped you ...

_ _ _ _ _ Breathe?

_ _ _ _ _ Distract yourself?

_ _ _ _ _ Soothe yourself?

_ _ _ _ _ Relax your body?

_ _ _ _ _ Change your thinking?

_ _ _ _ _ Or something else? _ _ _ _ _ _ _ _ _ _ _ _ _ _ _ _ _

Number these categories from 1 (most helpful) to 6 (least helpful)
or just circle your favorites.

Were there any specific prompts that stood out as really helpful or fun? List them here:

If you lowered your anxiety by working in this book—even just a little—let this fact empower and encourage you! Because it wasn't the prompts or the book or the author or whoever gave you the book that made this happen—it was *you*. You took the time to calm yourself; you took a risk and tried something new; you knocked those birds of worry and care right out of your hair!

And if you did it once, you can do it again! Be gentle with yourself, but persist. Anxiety is a sly dog, but it can be tamed! Learn what works for you, use what works for you, and don't give up. Sometimes it's the last key on the ring that opens the door!

Note to therapists, counselors, nurses, or anyone working with anxious adults:

As anxiety levels in the general population continue to rise, anxiety management tools and resources become more valuable than ever. *Put Your Anxiety Here* is the third in an innovative series of books containing creative and engaging, evidence-based journaling prompts that provide "therapy that doesn't look like therapy." The prompts in this book are designed specifically to help readers both release anxiety in the moment and learn techniques to manage it over time. All prompts are clinically based and grounded in principles of Cognitive Behavioral Therapy, Dialectical Behavior Therapy, mindfulness-based therapies, experiential therapies, or neuroscience.

This journal can be used by a reader on their own or as an adjunct to counseling or psychotherapy. It lends itself both to individual and group settings and can help the average anxious person, the hard-to-reach client, and those uncomfortable with traditional talk therapy.

Where direct questioning and exploration can sometimes feel threatening, journaling prompts are more subtle and can bypass defenses. When used during times of stress, the journal can interrupt the anxiety cycle and help relieve physical and emotional symptoms. The prompts in this journal are designed to change unhealthy thinking and breathing patterns, release physical tension, increase endorphin flow, strengthen neural pathways for peace, and empower the anxious person. Creative prompts can help people identify anxiety triggers, develop coping skills, and regulate emotions while still maintaining comfort with the process.

MORE >

To download a clinician's guide to using this book specifically, and journaling as an adjunct to therapy generally, please visit http://www.newharbinger.com/51451. If you are interested in earning continuing education credits for Lisa Schab's course on journaling as an adjunct to therapy, please visit http://www.pdrescources.org.

Acknowledgments

Thank you so very much!

To Tesilya Hanauer and Madison Davis who trust my words; to Amy Shoup and Sara Christian who give those words such beautiful energy and life; to Amy Blue who so willingly continues to seek and find.

Thank you to Tanya, Carol, Lisa D., Gertrude, and Betsy, from whom I gleaned ideas.

And tremendous thanks to The Muses who continue to whisper in my ear!

Lisa M. Schab

Real change *is* possible

For more than forty-five years, New Harbinger has published proven-effective self-help books and pioneering workbooks to help readers of all ages and backgrounds improve mental health and well-being, and achieve lasting personal growth. In addition, our spirituality books offer profound guidance for deepening awareness and cultivating healing, self-discovery, and fulfillment.

Founded by psychologist Matthew McKay and Patrick Fanning, New Harbinger is proud to be an independent, employee-owned company. Our books reflect our core values of integrity, innovation, commitment, sustainability, compassion, and trust. Written by leaders in the field and recommended by therapists worldwide, New Harbinger books are practical, accessible, and provide real tools for real change.

● newharbingerpublications

Lisa M. Schab, LCSW, is a practicing psychotherapist in the greater Chicago, IL, area; and author of eighteen self-help books, including *The Anxiety Workbook for Teens*, and the teen guided journals, *Put Your Worries Here* and *Put Your Feelings Here*. She has been interviewed as an expert on the Milwaukee television stations WTMJ-TV and WISN-TV, by *The New York Times*, *Scholastic Choices* magazine, *Teen Vogue*, *Psych Central*, and Kate Shannon's *Creative Therapy Umbrella* podcast. Schab has authored regular mental health columns for *Chicago Parent Magazine* and *The Sun Newspapers*. She is a member of the National Association of Social Workers (NASW).

You can find out more about her at www.lisamschabooks.com.

More Books from
New Harbinger Publications

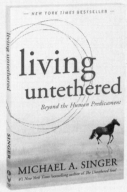

978-1648480935 / $18.95

978-1572246768 / $18.95

978-1684037858 / $18.95

978-1648480157 / $18.95

🌱 **newharbinger**publications

1-800-748-6273 / newharbinger.com